FLUTE

101 WORSHIP SONGS

MW00851724

Available for
FLUTE, CLARINET, ALTO SAX, TRUMPET, VIOLIN

ISBN 978-1-70512-271-6

Copyright © 2023 by HAL LEONARD LLC
International Copyright Secured All Rights Reserved

No part of this publication may be reproduced in any form or by
any means without the prior written permission of the Publisher.

Visit Hal Leonard Online at **www.halleonard.com**

Explore the entire family of Hal Leonard products and resources

World headquarters, contact:
Hal Leonard
7777 West Bluemound Road
Milwaukee, WI 53213
Email: info@halleonard.com

In Europe, contact:
Hal Leonard Europe Limited
1 Red Place
London, W1K 6PL
Email: info@halleonardeurope.com

In Australia, contact:
Hal Leonard Australia Pty. Ltd.
4 Lentara Court
Cheltenham, Victoria, 3192 Australia
Email: info@halleonard.com.au

CONTENTS

ABOVE ALL

FLUTE

© 1999 INTEGRITY'S HOSANNA! MUSIC (ASCAP) and LENSONGS PUBLISHING (ASCAP)
INTEGRITY'S HOSANNA! MUSIC Admin. at INTEGRATEDRIGHTS.COM
All Rights Reserved   Used by Permission

Words and Music by PAUL BALOCHE
and LENNY LeBLANC

Worshipfully

AMAZING GRACE
(My Chains Are Gone)

Flute

© 2006 worshiptogether.com Songs (ASCAP), sixsteps Music (ASCAP) and VAMOS PUBLISHING (ASCAP)
Admin. at CAPITOLCMGPUBLISHING.COM
All Rights Reserved   Used by Permission

Words by JOHN NEWTON
Traditional American Melody
Additional Words and Music by CHRIS TOMLIN
and LOUIE GIGLIO

ANOTHER IN THE FIRE

FLUTE

© 2019 HILLSONG MP SONGS (BMI)
Admin. in the United States and Canada at CAPITOLCMGPUBLISHING.COM
All Rights Reserved   Used by Permission

Words and Music by
CHRIS DAVENPORT

Worship Ballad

ANCIENT WORDS

FLUTE

© 2001 INTEGRITY'S HOSANNA! MUSIC (ASCAP)
Admin. at INTEGRATEDRIGHTS.COM
All Rights Reserved   Used by Permission

Words and Music by
LYNN DeSHAZO

AT THE CROSS
(Love Ran Red)

Flute

© 2014 THANKYOU MUSIC (PRS), ATLAS MOUNTAIN SONGS (BMI), worshiptogether.com Songs (ASCAP),
 WORSHIP TOGETHER MUSIC (BMI), sixsteps Music (ASCAP), sixsteps Songs (BMI),
 SAID AND DONE MUSIC (ASCAP), S.D.G. PUBLISHING (BMI),
 UNIVERSAL MUSIC - BRENTWOOD BENSON SONGS (BMI),
 UNIVERSAL MUSIC - BRENTWOOD BENSON TUNES (SESAC), COUNTLESS WONDER PUBLISHING (SESAC),
 FOTS MUSIC (SESAC) and McKITTRICK MUSIC (BMI)
THANKYOU MUSIC Admin. Worldwide at CAPITOLCMGPUBLISHING.COM excluding Europe which is Admin. by
 INTEGRITY MUSIC, part of the DAVID C COOK family. SONGS@INTEGRITYMUSIC.COM
ATLAS MOUNTAIN SONGS, worshiptogether.com Songs, WORSHIP TOGETHER MUSIC, sixsteps Music,
 sixsteps Songs, SAID AND DONE MUSIC, S.D.G. PUBLISHING, UNIVERSAL MUSIC - BRENTWOOD BENSON SONGS,
 UNIVERSAL MUSIC - BRENTWOOD BENSON TUNES, COUNTLESS WONDER PUBLISHING, FOTS MUSIC
 and McKITTRICK MUSIC Admin. at CAPITOLCMGPUBLISHING.COM
All Rights Reserved   Used by Permission

Words and Music by MATT REDMAN,
JONAS MYRIN, CHRIS TOMLIN,
ED CASH and MATT ARMSTRONG

BATTLE BELONGS

FLUTE

Copyright © 2020 Phil Wickham Music, Simply Global Songs and Bethel Music Publishing
All Rights for Phil Wickham Music and Simply Global Songs Admin. at EssentialMusicPublishing.com
All Rights Reserved   Used by Permission

Words and Music by PHIL WICKHAM
and BRIAN JOHNSON

Moderate Rock feel

BECAUSE HE LIVES, AMEN

FLUTE

© 2014 HANNA STREET MUSIC (BMI), worshiptogether.com Songs (ASCAP),
WORSHIP TOGETHER MUSIC (BMI), sixsteps Music (ASCAP), sixsteps Songs (BMI),
CAPITOL CMG PARAGON (BMI), S.D.G. PUBLISHING (BMI), BE ESSENTIAL SONGS (BMI),
I AM A PILGRIM SONGS (BMI), SO ESSENTIAL TUNES (SESAC) and OPEN HANDS MUSIC (SESAC)
HANNA STREET MUSIC, worshiptogether.com Songs, WORSHIP TOGETHER MUSIC, sixsteps Music,
sixsteps Songs, CAPITOL CMG PARAGON and S.D.G. PUBLISHING Admin. at CAPITOLCMGPUBLISHING.COM
BE ESSENTIAL SONGS, I AM A PILGRIM SONGS, SO ESSENTIAL TUNES and OPEN HANDS MUSIC
Admin. at ESSENTIALMUSICPUBLISHING.COM
All Rights Reserved   Used by Permission

Words and Music by WILLIAM J. GAITHER,
GLORIA GAITHER, DANIEL CARSON,
CHRIS TOMLIN, ED CASH,
MATT MAHER and JASON INGRAM

AS THE DEER

© 1984 UNIVERSAL MUSIC - BRENTWOOD BENSON PUBLISHING (ASCAP)
Admin. at CAPITOLCMGPUBLISHING.COM
All Rights Reserved   Used by Permission

Words and Music by
MARTIN NYSTROM

BLESSED BE YOUR NAME

Flute

© 2002 THANKYOU MUSIC (PRS)
Admin. Worldwide at CAPITOLCMGPUBLISHING.COM excluding Europe
which is Admin. by INTEGRITY MUSIC, part of the DAVID C COOK family. SONGS@INTEGRITYMUSIC.COM
All Rights Reserved   Used by Permission

Words and Music by MATT REDMAN
and BETH REDMAN

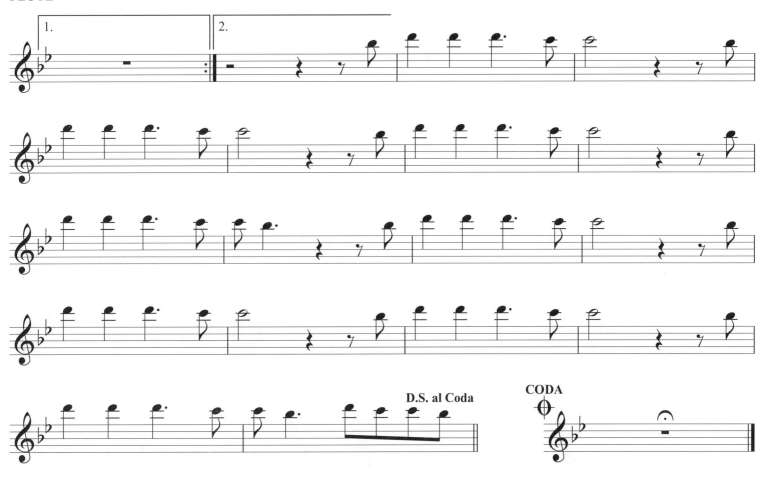

BEFORE THE THRONE OF GOD ABOVE

© 1997 SOVEREIGN GRACE WORSHIP (ASCAP)
Admin. at INTEGRATEDRIGHTS.COM
All Rights Reserved   Used by Permission

Words and Music by VIKKI COOK
and CHARITIE BANCROFT

With reverence

THE BLESSING

Flute

© 2020 WRITERS ROOF PUBLISHING (BMI), WORSHIP TOGETHER MUSIC (BMI),
CAPITOL CMG PARAGON (BMI), KARI JOBE CARNES MUSIC (BMI)
and MUSIC BY ELEVATION WORSHIP PUBLISHING (BMI)
WRITERS ROOF PUBLISHING, WORSHIP TOGETHER MUSIC, CAPITOL CMG PARAGON
and KARI JOBE CARNES MUSIC Admin. at CAPITOLCMGPUBLISHING.COM
MUSIC BY ELEVATION WORSHIP PUBLISHING Admin. at ESSENTIALMUSICPUBLISHING.COM
All Rights Reserved   Used by Permission

Words and Music by KARI JOBE CARNES,
CODY CARNES, STEVEN FURTICK
and CHRIS BROWN

BREATHE

FLUTE

© 1995 MERCY VINEYARD PUBLISHING (ASCAP)
Admin. at INTEGRATEDRIGHTS.COM
All Rights Reserved   Used by Permission

Words and Music by
MARIE BARNETT

With emotion

BROKEN VESSELS
(Amazing Grace)

FLUTE

© 2014 HILLSONG MUSIC PUBLISHING (APRA)
Admin. in the United States and Canada at CAPITOLCMGPUBLISHING.COM
All Rights Reserved   Used by Permission

Words and Music by JOEL HOUSTON
and JONAS MYRIN

Moderately

(small note optional)

BUILD MY LIFE

Flute

© 2016 THANKYOU MUSIC (PRS), HOUSEFIRES SOUNDS (ASCAP), worshiptogether.com Songs (ASCAP),
sixsteps Music (ASCAP), SAID AND DONE MUSIC (ASCAP), CAPITOL CMG GENESIS (ASCAP),
SENTRIC MUSIC LIMITED o/b/o ARKYARD MUSIC SERVICES LIMITED and BETHEL MUSIC PUBLISHING
THANKYOU MUSIC Admin. Worldwide at CAPITOLCMGPUBLISHING.COM excluding Europe which is Admin. by
 INTEGRITY MUSIC, a part of the DAVID C COOK family. SONGS@INTEGRITYMUSIC.COM
HOUSEFIRES SOUNDS, worshiptogether.com Songs, sixsteps Music, SAID AND DONE MUSIC
 and CAPITOL CMG GENESIS Admin. at CAPITOLCMGPUBLISHING.COM
All Rights Reserved   Used by Permission

Words and Music by MATT REDMAN,
PAT BARRETT, BRETT YOUNKER,
KARL MARTIN and KIRBY KAPLE

BUILD YOUR KINGDOM HERE

FLUTE

© 2012 THANKYOU MUSIC (PRS)
Admin. Worldwide at CAPITOLCMGPUBLISHING.COM excluding Europe which is Admin. by
INTEGRITYMUSIC.COM, part of the DAVID C COOK family, SONGS@INTEGRITYMUSIC.COM
All Rights Reserved   Used by Permission

Words and Music by
REND COLLECTIVE

COME, NOW IS THE TIME TO WORSHIP

FLUTE

© 1998 VINEYARD SONGS (UK/EIRE) (PRS)
Admin. at INTEGRATEDRIGHTS.COM
All Rights Reserved   Used by Permission

Words and Music by
BRIAN DOERKSEN

CHRIST OUR HOPE IN LIFE AND DEATH

FLUTE

© 2020 GETTY MUSIC PUBLISHING (BMI), MESSENGER HYMNS (BMI),
JORDAN KAUFLIN MUSIC (BMI), MATTHEW MERKER MUSIC (BMI),
LOVE YOUR ENEMIES PUBLISHING (ASCAP) and GETTY MUSIC HYMNS AND SONGS (ASCAP)
All Rights Admin. by MUSIC SERVICES
All Rights Reserved   Used by Permission

Words and Music by KEITH GETTY,
MATT BOSWELL, JORDAN KAUFLIN,
MATTHEW MERKER and MATT PAPA

GLORIFY THY NAME

© 1976 CCCM MUSIC (ASCAP) and UNIVERSAL MUSIC - BRENTWOOD BENSON PUBLISHING (ASCAP)
Copyright Renewed
Admin. at CAPITOLCMGPUBLISHING.COM
All Rights Reserved   Used by Permission

Words and Music by
DONNA W. ADKINS

Warmly

COME THOU FOUNT, COME THOU KING

FLUTE

© 2005 GATEWAY CREATE PUBLISHING
Admin. at INTEGRATEDRIGHTS.COM
All Rights Reserved   Used by Permission

Traditional
Additional Words and Music by
THOMAS MILLER

Moderately

CORNERSTONE

FLUTE

© 2012 HILLSONG MUSIC PUBLISHING (APRA)
Admin. in the United States and Canada at CAPITOLCMGPUBLISHING.COM
All Rights Reserved   Used by Permission

Words and Music by JONAS MYRIN,
REUBEN MORGAN, ERIC LILJERO
and EDWARD MOTE

Moderately

DAYS OF ELIJAH

FLUTE

© 1996 Daybreak Music, Ltd. (Admin. by Song Solutions CopyCare,
  excluding US and Canada admin. by Music Services, Inc. www.musicservices.org)
All Rights Reserved   Used by Permission

Words and Music by
ROBIN MARK

GREAT IS THE LORD

© 1982 MEADOWGREEN MUSIC COMPANY (ASCAP)
Admin. at CAPITOLCMGPUBLISHING.COM
All Rights Reserved   Used by Permission

Words and Music by MICHAEL W. SMITH
and DEBORAH D. SMITH

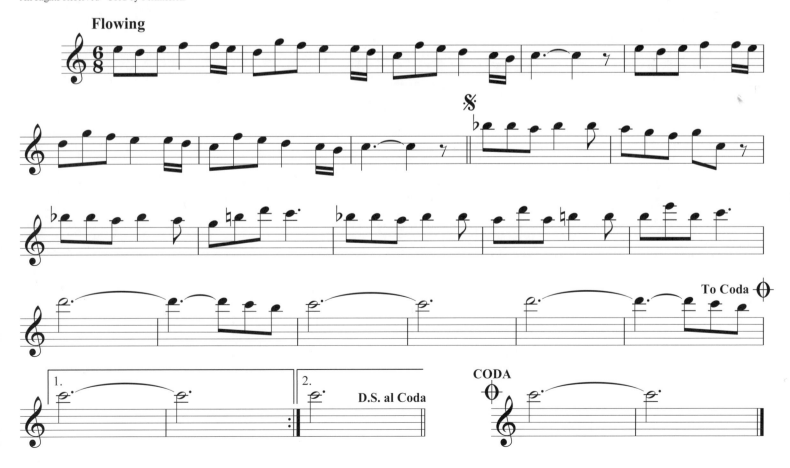

DO IT AGAIN

Flute

© 2016 THANKYOU MUSIC (PRS), worshiptogether.com Songs (ASCAP), sixsteps Music (ASCAP),
   SAID AND DONE MUSIC (ASCAP) and MUSIC BY ELEVATION WORSHIP PUBLISHING (BMI)
THANKYOU MUSIC Admin. Worldwide at CAPITOLCMGPUBLISHING.COM excluding Europe which is Admin. by
   INTEGRITY MUSIC, part of the David C Cook family. SONGS@INTEGRITYMUSIC.COM
worshiptogether.com Songs, sixsteps Music and SAID AND DONE MUSIC Admin. at CAPITOLCMGPUBLISHING.COM
MUSIC BY ELEVATION WORSHIP PUBLISHING Admin. at ESSENTIALMUSICPUBLISHING.COM
All Rights Reserved   Used by Permission

Words and Music by MATT REDMAN,
STEVEN FURTICK, CHRIS BROWN
and MACK BROCK

HOW DEEP THE FATHER'S LOVE FOR US

© 1995 THANKYOU MUSIC (PRS)
Admin. Worldwide at CAPITOLCMGPUBLISHING.COM excluding Europe which is Admin. by
INTEGRITY MUSIC, part of the DAVID C COOK family. SONGS@INTEGRITYMUSIC.COM
All Rights Reserved   Used by Permission

Words and Music by
STUART TOWNEND

DRAW ME CLOSE

FLUTE

© 1994 MERCY VINEYARD PUBLISHING (ASCAP)
Admin. at INTEGRATEDRIGHTS.COM
All Rights Reserved   Used by Permission

Words and Music by
KELLY CARPENTER

EVERLASTING GOD

FLUTE

© 2005 THANKYOU MUSIC (PRS)
Admin. Worldwide at CAPITOLCMGPUBLISHING.COM excluding Europe which is Admin. by
INTEGRITY MUSIC, part of the DAVID C COOK family. SONGS@INTEGRITYMUSIC.COM
All Rights Reserved   Used by Permission

Words and Music by BRENTON BROWN
and KEN RILEY

FOREVER

FLUTE

© 2001 WORSHIPTOGETHER.COM SONGS (ASCAP) and sixsteps Music (ASCAP)
Admin. at CAPITOLCMGPUBLISHING.COM
All Rights Reserved   Used by Permission

Words and Music by
CHRIS TOMLIN

FOREVER REIGN

FLUTE

Copyright © 2009 Spirit Catalog Holdings, S.a.r.l., So Essential Tunes,
Spirit Nashville Three (formerly West Main Music) and Hillsong Music Publishing
All Rights for Spirit Catalog Holdings, S.a.r.l. Controlled and Administered by Spirit Nashville Three
All Rights for So Essential Tunes and Spirit Nashville Three (formerly West Main Music)
 Administered at EssentialMusicPublishing.com
All Rights for Hillsong Music Publishing Administered in the United States and Canada at CapitolCMGPublishing.com
All Rights Reserved   Used by Permission

Words and Music by JASON INGRAM
and REUBEN MORGAN

GIVE THANKS

FLUTE

© 1978 INTEGRITY'S HOSANNA! MUSIC (ASCAP)
Admin. at INTEGRATEDRIGHTS.COM
All Rights Reserved   Used by Permission

Words and Music by
HENRY SMITH

GOOD GRACE

Flute

© 2018 HILLSONG MP SONGS (BMI)
Admin. in the United States and Canada at CAPITOLCMGPUBLISHING.COM
All Rights Reserved   Used by Permission

Words and Music by
JOEL HOUSTON

Moderately slow

GLORIOUS DAY

Flute

© 2017 SOUNDS OF JERICHO (BMI), KRISTIAN STANFILL PUBLISHING DESIGNEE (NS),
  worshiptogether.com Songs (ASCAP), WORSHIP TOGETHER MUSIC (BMI),
  sixsteps Music (ASCAP), sixsteps Songs (BMI), FELLOW SHIPS MUSIC (SESAC),
  SO ESSENTIAL TUNES (SESAC) and HICKORY BILL DOC (SESAC)
SOUNDS OF JERICHO, KRISTIAN STANFILL PUBLISHING DESIGNEE, worshiptogether.com Songs,
  WORSHIP TOGETHER MUSIC, sixsteps Music and sixsteps Songs Admin. at CAPITOLCMGPUBLISHING.COM
FELLOW SHIPS MUSIC, SO ESSENTIAL TUNES and HICKORY BILL DOC Admin. at ESSENTIALMUSICPUBLISHING.COM
All Rights Reserved   Used by Permission

Words and Music by SEAN CURRAN,
KRISTIAN STANFILL, JASON INGRAM
and JONATHAN SMITH

With energy

GOOD GOOD FATHER

Flute

© 2014 COMMON HYMNAL DIGITAL (BMI), HOUSEFIRES SOUNDS (ASCAP),
TONY BROWN PUBLISHING DESIGNEE (BMI), worshiptogether.com Songs (ASCAP),
sixsteps Music (ASCAP), VAMOS PUBLISHING (ASCAP) and CAPITOL CMG PARAGON (BMI)
Admin. at CAPITOLCMGPUBLISHING.COM
All Rights Reserved   Used by Permission

Words and Music by PAT BARRETT
and ANTHONY BROWN

GOODNESS OF GOD

Flute

© 2019 SHOUT! MUSIC PUBLISHING (APRA), ALLETROP MUSIC (BMI), FELLOW SHIPS MUSIC (SESAC),
   SO ESSENTIAL TUNES (SESAC) and BETHEL MUSIC PUBLISHING
SHOUT! MUSIC PUBLISHING Admin. in the United States and Canada at CAPITOLCMGPUBLISHING.COM
ALLETROP MUSIC Admin. at CAPITOLCMGPUBLISHING.COM
FELLOW SHIPS MUSIC and SO ESSENTIAL TUNES Admin. at ESSENTIALMUSICPUBLISHING.COM
All Rights Reserved   Used by Permission

Words and Music by BEN FIELDING,
ED CASH, JASON INGRAM,
JENN JOHNSON and BRIAN JOHNSON

GRAVES INTO GARDENS

Flute

Copyright © 2020 Music By Elevation Worship Publishing, Bethel Music Publishing
  and Maverick City Publishing Worldwide (Admin. by Heritage Worship Publishing)
All Rights for Music By Elevation Worship Publishing Administered at EssentialMusicPublishing.com
All Rights for Heritage Worship Publishing Administered by Bethel Music Publishing
All Rights Reserved   Used by Permission

Words and Music by CHRIS BROWN,
STEVEN FURTICK, TIFFANY HAMMER
and BRANDON LAKE

GREAT I AM

FLUTE

© 2011 INTEGRITY WORSHIP MUSIC (ASCAP)
Admin. at INTEGRATEDRIGHTS.COM
All Rights Reserved   Used by Permission

Words and Music by
JARED ANDERSON

Moderate Pop beat

GREAT THINGS

FLUTE

Copyright © 2018 Phil Wickham Music, Simply Global Songs,
 Sing My Songs, Son Of The Lion and Capitol CMG Paragon
All Rights for Phil Wickham Music, Simply Global Songs
 and Sing My Songs Admin. at EssentialMusicPublishing.com
All Rights for Song Of The Lion and Capitol CMG Paragon Admin. at CapitolCMGPublishing.com
All Rights Reserved   Used by Permission

Words and Music by JONAS MYRIN
and PHIL WICKHAM

Moderate Rock beat

GREAT ARE YOU LORD

FLUTE

Copyright © 2013 Open Hands Music, So Essential Tunes, Integrity's Praise! Music and Little Way Creative
All Rights for Open Hands Music and So Essential Tunes Administered at EssentialMusicPublishing.com
All Rights for Integrity's Praise! Music and Little Way Creative Administered at IntegratedRights.com
International Copyright Secured   All Rights Reserved

Words and Music by JASON INGRAM,
DAVID LEONARD and LESLIE JORDAN

THE HEART OF WORSHIP
(When the Music Fades)

FLUTE

© 1999 THANKYOU MUSIC (PRS)
Admin. Worldwide at CAPITOLCMGPUBLISHING.COM excluding Europe which is Admin. by
 INTEGRITYMUSIC.COM, part of the DAVID C COOK family. SONGS @INTEGRITYMUSIC.COM
All Rights Reserved   Used by Permission

Words and Music by
MATT REDMAN

Steady Ballad

HERE I AM TO WORSHIP
(Light of the World)

FLUTE

© 2001 THANKYOU MUSIC (PRS)
Admin. Worldwide at CAPITOLCMGPUBLISHING.COM excluding Europe which is Admin. by
 INTEGRITYMUSIC.COM, part of the DAVID C COOK family. SONGS@INTEGRITYMUSIC.COM
All Rights Reserved   Used by Permission

Words and Music by
TIM HUGHES

Moderately slow, steady

HIS MERCY IS MORE

FLUTE

© 2015 MESSENGER HYMNS (BMI), GETTY MUSIC PUBLISHING (BMI),
 GETTY MUSIC HYMNS AND SONGS (ASCAP) and LOVE YOUR ENEMIES PUBLISHING (ASCAP)
All Rights Admin. by MUSIC SERVICES
All Rights Reserved   Used by Permission

Words and Music by MATT BOSWELL
and MATT PAPA

Slow Gospel feel

HOLY IS THE LORD

FLUTE

© 2003 WORSHIPTOGETHER.COM SONGS (ASCAP) and sixsteps Music (ASCAP)
Admin. at CAPITOLCMGPUBLISHING.COM
All Rights Reserved   Used by Permission

Words and Music by CHRIS TOMLIN
and LOUIE GIGLIO

HOSANNA
(Praise Is Rising)

FLUTE

© 2006 INTEGRITY'S HOSANNA! MUSIC (ASCAP) and THANKYOU MUSIC LTD. (PRS)
INTEGRITY'S HOSANNA! MUSIC Admin. at INTEGRATEDRIGHTS.COM
THANKYOU MUSIC LTD. Admin. Worldwide at CAPITOLCMGPUBLISHING.COM
 excluding UK and Europe which is Admin. at INTEGRATEDRIGHTS.COM
All Rights Reserved   Used by Permission

Words and Music by PAUL BALOCHE
and BRENTON BROWN

Moderately fast

HOLY SPIRIT

FLUTE

© 2011 JESUS CULTURE MUSIC (ASCAP) and CAPITOL CMG GENESIS (ASCAP)
Admin. at CAPITOLCMGPUBLISHING.COM
All Rights Reserved   Used by Permission

Words and Music by KATIE TORWALT
and BRYAN TORWALT

Worship Ballad

HE IS EXALTED

© 1985 STRAIGHTWAY MUSIC (ASCAP) and MOUNTAIN SPRING MUSIC (ASCAP)
Admin. at CAPITOLCMGPUBLISHING.COM
All Rights Reserved   Used by Permission

Words and Music by
TWILA PARIS

Flowing, in 2

HOUSE OF THE LORD

FLUTE

Copyright © 2021 Phil Wickham Music, Simply Global Songs, Cashagamble Jet Music and Be Essential Songs
All Rights Admin. at EssentialMusicPublishing.com
All Rights Reserved   Used by Permission

Words and Music by PHIL WICKHAM
and JONATHAN SMITH

D.S. al Coda

CODA

HOW GREAT IS OUR GOD

Flute

© 2004 worshiptogether.com Songs (ASCAP), sixsteps Music (ASCAP)
 and WONDROUSLY MADE SONGS (BMI) (a division of Wondrous Worship & Llano Music, LLC)
worshiptogether.com Songs and sixsteps Music Admin. at CAPITOLCMGPUBLISHING.COM
WONDROUSLY MADE SONGS (a division of Wondrous Worship & Llano Music, LLC) Admin. by MUSIC SERVICES
All Rights Reserved   Used by Permission

Words and Music by CHRIS TOMLIN,
JESSE REEVES and ED CASH

Moderately slow

I GIVE YOU MY HEART

FLUTE

© 1995 HILLSONG PUBLISHING (ASCAP)
Admin. in the United States and Canada at CAPITOLCMGPUBLISHING.COM
All Rights Reserved   Used by Permission

Words and Music by
REUBEN MORGAN

Moderately

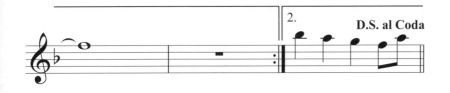

I WILL RISE

Flute

© 2008 WORSHIPTOGETHER.COM SONGS (ASCAP), sixsteps Music (ASCAP),
VAMOS PUBLISHING (ASCAP), SPIRITANDSONG.COM PUBLISHING (BMI) and THANKYOU MUSIC (PRS)
WORSHIPTOGETHER.COM SONGS, sixsteps Music, VAMOS PUBLISHING
and SPIRITANDSONG.COM PUBLISHING Admin. at CAPITOLCMGPUBLISHING.COM
THANKYOU MUSIC Admin. Worldwide at CAPITOLCMGPUBLISHING.COM excluding Europe which is Admin. by
INTEGRITYMUSIC.COM, part of the DAVID C COOK family, SONGS@INTEGRITYMUSIC.COM
All Rights Reserved   Used by Permission

Words and Music by CHRIS TOMLIN,
JESSE REEVES, LOUIE GIGLIO
and MATT MAHER

IN CHRIST ALONE

© 2002 THANKYOU MUSIC (PRS)
Admin. Worldwide at CAPITOLCMGPUBLISHING.COM excluding Europe which is Admin. by
INTEGRITY MUSIC, part of the DAVID C COOK family. SONGS@INTEGRITYMUSIC.COM
All Rights Reserved   Used by Permission

Words and Music by KEITH GETTY
and STUART TOWNEND

Moderately slow

INDESCRIBABLE

FLUTE

© 2004 LAURA STORIES (ASCAP), worshiptogether.com Songs (ASCAP) and sixsteps Music (ASCAP)
Admin. at CAPITOLCMGPUBLISHING.COM
All Rights Reserved   Used by Permission

Words and Music by LAURA STORY
and JESSE REEVES

With motion, in 2

LORD, I NEED YOU

Flute

© 2011 THANKYOU MUSIC (PRS), worshiptogether.com Songs (ASCAP), sixsteps Music (ASCAP),
  SWEATER WEATHER MUSIC (ASCAP) and VALLEY OF SONGS MUSIC (BMI)
THANKYOU MUSIC Admin. Worldwide at CAPITOLCMGPUBLISHING.COM
  excluding Europe which is Admin. by INTEGRITY MUSIC, part of the DAVID C COOK family.
SONGS@INTEGRITYMUSIC.COM
worshiptogether.com Songs, sixsteps Music, SWEATER WEATHER MUSIC and VALLEY OF SONGS MUSIC
  Admin. at CAPITOLCMGPUBLISHING.COM
All Rights Reserved   Used by Permission

Words and Music by JESSE REEVES,
KRISTIAN STANFILL, MATT MAHER,
CHRISTY NOCKELS and DANIEL CARSON

IS HE WORTHY?

FLUTE

© 2018 JAKEDOG MUSIC, VAMOS PUBLISHING, CAPITOL CMG GENESIS and JUNKBOX MUSIC
JAKEDOG MUSIC Admin. by MUSIC SERVICES
VAMOS PUBLISHING and CAPITOL CMG GENESIS Admin. at CAPITOLCMGPUBLISHING.COM
JUNKBOX MUSIC Admin. by SONGS OF RAZOR AND TIE c/o CONCORD MUSIC PUBLISHING
All Rights Reserved   Used by Permission

Words and Music by ANDREW PETERSON
and BEN SHIVE

Gentle Ballad

JESUS MESSIAH

FLUTE

© 2008 worshiptogether.com Songs (ASCAP), sixsteps Music (ASCAP), VAMOS PUBLISHING (ASCAP)
 and WONDROUSLY MADE SONGS (BMI) (a division of Wondrous Worship & Llano Music, LLC)
worshiptogether.com songs, sixsteps Music and VAMOS PUBLISHING Admin. at CAPITOLCMGPUBLISHING.COM
WONDROUSLY MADE SONGS (a division of Wondrous Worship & Llano Music, LLC) Admin. by MUSIC SERVICES
All Rights Reserved   Used by Permission

Words and Music by CHRIS TOMLIN,
JESSE REEVES, DANIEL CARSON
and ED CASH

Moderately

KING OF KINGS

FLUTE

© 2019 HILLSONG MP SONGS (ASCAP), FELLOW SHIPS MUSIC (SESAC)
 and SO ESSENTIAL TUNES (SESAC)
HILLSONG MP SONGS Admin. in the United States and Canada at CAPITOLCMGPUBLISHING.COM
FELLOW SHIPS MUSIC and SO ESSENTIAL TUNES Admin. at ESSENTIALMUSICPUBLISHING.COM
All Rights Reserved   Used by Permission

Words and Music by SCOTT LIGERTWOOD,
BROOKE LIGERTWOOD and JASON INGRAM

KING OF MY HEART

FLUTE

© 2015 MEAUX JEAUX MUSIC (SESAC), RAUCOUS RUCKUS PUBLISHING (SESAC)
   and WATERSHED MUSIC GROUP (SESAC)
MEAUX JEAUX MUSIC and RAUCOUS RUCKUS PUBLISHING
   Admin. at CAPITOLCMGPUBLISHING.COM
All Rights Reserved   Used by Permission

Words and Music by JOHN MARK McMILLAN
and SARAH McMILLAN

LAMB OF GOD

© 1985 STRAIGHTWAY MUSIC (ASCAP) and MOUNTAIN SPRING MUSIC (ASCAP)
Admin. at CAPITOLCMGPUBLISHING.COM
All Rights Reserved   Used by Permission

Words and Music by
TWILA PARIS

With emotion

THE LION AND THE LAMB

flute

© 2015 THANKYOU MUSIC (PRS), MEAUX MERCY (BMI), THE DEVIL IS A LIAR! PUBLISHING (BMI)
  and BETHEL MUSIC PUBLISHING (ASCAP)
THANKYOU MUSIC Admin. Worldwide at CAPITOLCMGPUBLISHING.COM
  excluding Europe which is Admin. by INTEGRITY MUSIC, part of the DAVID C COOK family.
SONGS@INTEGRITYMUSIC.COM
MEAUX MERCY and THE DEVIL IS A LIAR! PUBLISHING Admin. at CAPITOLCMGPUBLISHING.COM
All Rights Reserved   Used by Permission

Words and Music by BRENTON BROWN,
BRIAN JOHNSON and LEELAND MOORING

LIVING HOPE

FLUTE

Copyright © 2018 Sing My Songs, Phil Wickham Music, Simply Global Songs and Bethel Music Publishing
All Rights for Sing My Songs, Phil Wickham Music and Simply Global Songs Admin. at EssentialMusicPublishing.com
All Rights Reserved   Used by Permission

Words and Music by PHIL WICKHAM
and BRIAN JOHNSON

MORE PRECIOUS THAN SILVER

© 1982 INTEGRITY'S HOSANNA! MUSIC (ASCAP)
Admin. at INTEGRATEDRIGHTS.COM
All Rights Reserved   Used by Permission

Words and Music by
LYNN DeSHAZO

MAJESTY

FLUTE

© 1984 NEW SPRING PUBLISHING INC. (ASCAP)
Admin. at CAPITOLCMGPUBLISHING.COM
All Rights Reserved   Used by Permission

Words and Music by
JACK HAYFORD

MIGHTY TO SAVE

FLUTE

© 2006 HILLSONG MUSIC PUBLISHING (APRA)
Admin. in the United States and Canada at CAPITOLCMGPUBLISHING.COM
All Rights Reserved   Used by Permission

Words and Music by BEN FIELDING
and REUBEN MORGAN

NO LONGER SLAVES

FLUTE

Copyright © 2014 Bethel Music Publishing (ASCAP)
All Rights Reserved   Used by Permission

Words and Music by JONATHAN DAVID HELSER,
BRIAN JOHNSON and JOEL CASE

NOTHING ELSE

Flute

© 2019 WRITERS ROOF PUBLISHING (BMI), EVERY SQUARE INCH (SESAC), CAPITOL CMG PARAGON (BMI) and CAPITOL CMG AMPLIFIER (SESAC) Admin. at CAPITOLCMGPUBLISHING.COM
All Rights Reserved   Used by Permission

Words and Music by CODY CARNES, HANK BENTLEY and JESSIE EARLY

O COME TO THE ALTAR

Flute

Copyright © 2016 Music By Elevation Worship Publishing
All Rights Administered at EssentialMusicPublishing.com
All Rights Reserved   Used by Permission

Words and Music by CHRIS BROWN,
MACK BROCK, STEVEN FURTICK
and WADE JOYE

O CHURCH ARISE

Flute

© 2005 THANKYOU MUSIC (PRS)
Admin. Worldwide at CAPITOLCMGPUBLISHING.COM excluding Europe which is Admin. by
INTEGRITYMUSIC.COM, part of the DAVID C COOK family, SONGS@INTEGRITYMUSIC.COM
All Rights Reserved   Used by Permission

Words and Music by KEITH GETTY
and STUART TOWNEND

O PRAISE THE NAME
(Anástasis)

Flute

© 2015 HILLSONG MUSIC PUBLISHING (APRA)
Admin. in the United States and Canada at CAPITOLCMGPUBLISHING.COM
All Rights Reserved   Used by Permission

Words and Music by MARTY SAMPSON,
BENJAMIN HASTINGS and DEAN USSHER

OCEANS
(Where Feet May Fail)

FLUTE

© 2013 HILLSONG MUSIC PUBLISHING (APRA)
Admin. in the United States and Canada at CAPITOLCMGPUBLISHING.COM
All Rights Reserved   Used by Permission

Words and Music by JOEL HOUSTON,
MATT CROCKER and SALOMON LIGHTHELM

Moderately slow

LORD, I LIFT YOUR NAME ON HIGH

© 1989 UNIVERSAL MUSIC - BRENTWOOD BENSON PUBLISHING (ASCAP)
Admin. at CAPITOLCMGPUBLISHING.COM
All Rights Reserved   Used by Permission

Words and Music by
RICK FOUNDS

Brightly

ONLY KING FOREVER

FLUTE

Copyright © 2014 Be Essential Songs and Elevation Worship Publishing
All Rights Administered at EssentialMusicPublishing.com
International Copyright Secured   All Rights Reserved

Words and Music by MACK BROCK,
CHRISTOPHER BROWN, STEVEN FURTICK
and WADE JOYE

Joyfully, with a driving beat

ONE THING REMAINS
(Your Love Never Fails)

FLUTE

© 2010 MERCY VINEYARD PUBLISHING (ASCAP) (Admin. at INTEGRATEDRIGHTS.COM),
BETHEL MUSIC PUBLISHING (ASCAP) and CHRISTAJOY MUSIC (BMI)
 (Admin. by BETHEL MUSIC PUBLISHING)
All Rights Reserved   Used by Permission

Words and Music by JEREMY RIDDLE,
BRIAN JOHNSON and CHRISTA BLACK

OPEN THE EYES OF MY HEART

FLUTE

© 1997 INTEGRITY'S HOSANNA! MUSIC (ASCAP)
Admin. at INTEGRATEDRIGHTS.COM
All Rights Reserved   Used by Permission

Words and Music by
PAUL BALOCHE

OPEN UP THE HEAVENS

Flute

Copyright © 2012, 2013 HBC Worship Music, All Essential Music, So Essential Tunes,
  Open Hands Music, Stugio Music Publishing and Curb Songs
All Rights on behalf of HBC Worship Music, All Essential Music, So Essential Tunes,
  Open Hands Music and Stugio Music Publishing Administered at EssentialMusicPublishing.com
International Copyright Secured   All Rights Reserved

Words and Music by JASON INGRAM,
STUART GARRARD, ANDI ROZIER,
JAMES MACDONALD and MEREDITH ANDREWS

With anticipation

SHINE, JESUS, SHINE

FLUTE

© 1987 MAKE WAY MUSIC (ASCAP)
Admin. in the Western Hemisphere by MUSIC SERVICES
All Rights Reserved   Used by Permission

Words and Music by
GRAHAM KENDRICK

OUR GOD

Flute

© 2010 THANKYOU MUSIC (PRS), ATLAS MOUNTAIN SONGS (BMI),
 worshiptogether.com Songs (ASCAP), sixsteps Music (ASCAP) and VAMOS PUBLISHING (ASCAP)
THANKYOU MUSIC Admin. Worldwide at CAPITOLCMGPUBLISHING.COM excluding Europe which is Admin. by
 INTEGRITY MUSIC, part of the DAVID C COOK family. SONGS@INTEGRITYMUSIC.COM
ATLAS MOUNTAIN SONGS, worshiptogether.com Songs, sixsteps Music
 and VAMOS PUBLISHING Admin. at CAPITOLCMGPUBLISHING.COM
All Rights Reserved   Used by Permission

Words and Music by JONAS MYRIN,
JESSE REEVES, CHRIS TOMLIN
and MATT REDMAN

THE POWER OF THE CROSS
(Oh to See the Dawn)

© 2005 THANKYOU MUSIC (PRS)
Admin. Worldwide at CAPITOLCMGPUBLISHING.COM excluding Europe which is Admin. by
INTEGRITYMUSIC.COM, part of the DAVID C COOK family, SONGS@INTEGRITYMUSIC.COM
All Rights Reserved   Used by Permission

Words and Music by STUART TOWNEND
and KEITH GETTY

Moderately slow

RAISE A HALLELUJAH

FLUTE

Copyright © 2018 Bethel Music Publishing (ASCAP)
All Rights Reserved   Used by Permission

Words and Music by JONATHAN DAVID HELSER,
MELISSA HELSER, MOLLY SKAGGS
and JAKE STEVENS

Moderate Rock beat

RECKLESS LOVE

FLUTE

Copyright © 2017, 2018 Bethel Music Publishing (ASCAP), Watershed Publishing Group (ASCAP)
 and Richmond Park Publishing (BMI)
All Rights for Richmond Park Publishing Admin. at EssentialMusicPublishing.com
All Rights Reserved   Used by Permission

Words and Music by CALEB CULVER,
CORY ASBURY and RAN JACKSON

RESURRECTING

Flute

Copyright © 2016 Music By Elevation Worship Publishing
All Rights Administered at EssentialMusicPublishing.com
All Rights Reserved   Used by Permission

Words and Music by CHRIS BROWN,
MACK BROCK, STEVEN FURTICK,
WADE JOYE and MATTHEWS THABO NTELE

REVELATION SONG

FLUTE

© 2004 GATEWAY CREATE PUBLISHING (BMI)
Admin. at INTEGRATEDRIGHTS.COM
All Rights Reserved   Used by Permission

Words and Music by
JENNIE LEE RIDDLE

SHINE ON US

Copyright © 1996, 1998 Sony Music Publishing (US) LLC and Deer Valley Music
All Rights on behalf of Sony Music Publishing (US) LLC Administered by
 Sony Music Publishing (US) LLC, 424 Church Street, Suite 1200, Nashville, TN 37219
All Rights on behalf of Deer Valley Music Administered at
 CapitolCMGPublishing.com International Copyright Secured   All Rights Reserved

Words and Music by MICHAEL W. SMITH
and DEBBIE SMITH

RUN TO THE FATHER

Flute

Copyright © 2019 Be Essential Songs, Songs From Richmond Park,
 I Am A Pilgrim Songs, Writers Roof Publishing and Capitol CMG Paragon
All Rights for Be Essential Songs, Songs From Richmond Park
 and I Am A Pilgrim Songs Administered at EssentialMusicPublishing.com
All Rights for Writers Roof Publishing and Capitol CMG Paragon Administered at CapitolCMGPublishing.com
All Rights Reserved   Used by Permission

Words and Music by RAN JACKSON,
MATT MAHER and CODY CARNES

SEE A VICTORY

Flute

Copyright © 2019 Music By Elevation Worship Publishing, So Essential Tunes,
  Fellow Ships Music and SHOUT MP Brio
All Rights for Music By Elevation Worship Publishing, So Essential Tunes
  and Fellow Ships Music Administered at EssentialMusicPublishing.com
All Rights for SHOUT MP Brio Administered in the U.S. and Canada at CapitolCMGPublishing.com
All Rights Reserved   Used by Permission

Words and Music by CHRIS BROWN,
STEVEN FURTICK, JASON INGRAM
AND BEN FIELDING

SHOUT TO THE LORD

FLUTE

© 1993 WONDROUS WORSHIP (ASCAP)
Administered by MUSIC SERVICES o/b/o LLANO MUSIC LLC
All Rights Reserved   Used by Permission

Words and Music by
DARLENE ZSCHECH

SPEAK O LORD

FLUTE

© 2006 THANKYOU MUSIC (PRS)
Admin. Worldwide at CAPITOLCMGPUBLISHING.COM excluding Europe which is Admin. by
 INTEGRITY MUSIC, part of the David C. Cook family. SONGS@INTEGRITYMUSIC.COM
All Rights Reserved   Used by Permission

Words and Music by STUART TOWNEND
and KEITH GETTY

STEP BY STEP

© 1991 KID BROTHERS OF ST. FRANK (ASCAP)
 and UNIVERSAL MUSIC - BRENTWOOD BENSON PUBLISHING (ASCAP)
Admin. at CAPITOLCMGPUBLISHING.COM
All Rights Reserved   Used by Permission

Words and Music by
DAVID STRASSER "BEAKER"

THIS I BELIEVE
(The Creed)

FLUTE

© 2014 HILLSONG MUSIC PUBLISHING (APRA)
Admin. in the United States and Canada at CAPITOLCMGPUBLISHING.COM
All Rights Reserved   Used by Permission

Words and Music by BEN FIELDING
and MATT CROCKER

THERE IS A REDEEMER

© 1982 BIRDWING MUSIC (ASCAP), EARS TO HEAR MUSIC (ASCAP) and
UNIVERSAL MUSIC - BRENTWOOD BENSON PUBLISHING (ASCAP)
Admin. at CAPITOLCMGPUBLISHING.COM
All Rights Reserved   Used by Permission

Words and Music by
MELODY GREEN

THIS IS AMAZING GRACE

FLUTE

© 2012 SING MY SONGS (BMI), SEEMS LIKE MUSIC (BMI),
 PHIL WICKHAM MUSIC (BMI), WC MUSIC CORP. (ASCAP), JOSH'S MUSIC (ASCAP),
 FBR MUSIC (ASCAP) and BETHEL MUSIC PUBLISHING (ASCAP)
SING MY SONGS, SEEMS LIKE MUSIC and PHIL WICKHAM MUSIC Administered by
 BMG RIGHTS MANAGEMENT c/o MUSIC SERVICES
JOSH'S MUSIC and FBR MUSIC Administered by WC MUSIC CORP.
All Rights Reserved   Used by Permission

Words and Music by PHIL WICKHAM,
JOSHUA NEIL FARRO and JEREMY RIDDLE

Moderate Rock beat

10,000 REASONS
(Bless the Lord)

FLUTE

© 2011 ATLAS MOUNTAIN SONGS (BMI), worshiptogether.com Songs (ASCAP),
 sixsteps Music (ASCAP) and THANKYOU MUSIC (PRS)
ATLAS MOUNTAIN SONGS, worshiptogether.com Songs and sixsteps Music Admin. at CAPITOLCMGPUBLISHING.COM
THANKYOU MUSIC Admin. Worldwide at CAPITOLCMGPUBLISHING.COM excluding Europe which is Admin. by
 INTEGRITY MUSIC, part of the DAVID C COOK family. SONGS@INTEGRITYMUSIC.COM
All Rights Reserved   Used by Permission

Words and Music by JONAS MYRIN
and MATT REDMAN

Moderate Ballad

WHOM SHALL I FEAR
(God of Angel Armies)

FLUTE

© 2013 MCTYEIRE MUSIC (BMI), TWELVE LIONS MUSIC (BMI), WORSHIP TOGETHER MUSIC (BMI),
CAPITOL CMG PARAGON (BMI) and S.D.G. PUBLISHING (BMI)
Admin. at CAPITOLCMGPUBLISHING.COM All Rights Reserved   Used by Permission

Words and Music by CHRIS TOMLIN,
ED CASH and SCOTT CASH

WAY MAKER

FLUTE

© 2016 INTEGRITY MUSIC (PRS)
Admin. at INTEGRATEDRIGHTS.COM
All Rights Reserved   Used by Permission

Words and Music by
OSINACHI KALU OKORO EGBU

WHAT A BEAUTIFUL NAME

FLUTE

© 2016 HILLSONG MUSIC PUBLISHING (APRA)
Admin. in the United States and Canada at CAPITOLCMGPUBLISHING.COM
All Rights Reserved   Used by Permission

Words and Music by BEN FIELDING
and BROOKE LIGERTWOOD

Moderately slow

WHO YOU SAY I AM

FLUTE

© 2018 HILLSONG MUSIC PUBLISHING (APRA)
Admin. in the United States and Canada at CAPITOLCMGPUBLISHING.COM
All Rights Reserved   Used by Permission

Words and Music by REUBEN MORGAN
and BEN FIELDING

WORTHY IS THE LAMB

FLUTE

© 2000 WONDROUS WORSHIP (ASCAP)
Admin. by MUSIC SERVICES o/b/o LLANO MUSIC LLC
All Rights Reserved   Used by Permission

Words and Music by
DARLENE ZSCHECH

YES I WILL

Flute

Copyright © 2019 HBC Worship Music, All Essential Music, Upside Down Under,
 Be Essential Songs, Hickory Bill Doc, So Essential Tunes and Jingram Music Publishing
All Rights Administered at EssentialMusicPublishing.com

Words and Music by MIA FIELDES,
EDDIE HOAGLAND and JONATHAN SMITH

WE FALL DOWN

© 1998 WORSHIPTOGETHER.COM SONGS (ASCAP), sixsteps Music (ASCAP)
and VAMOS PUBLISHING (ASCAP)
Admin. at CAPITOLCMGPUBLISHING.COM
All Rights Reserved   Used by Permission

Words and Music by
CHRIS TOMLIN

Worshipfully

YOU ARE MY ALL IN ALL

© 1991 Shepherd's Heart Music, Inc. (Admin. by PraiseCharts Publishing, Inc.)
All Rights Reserved   Used by Permission

By DENNIS JERNIGAN

Moderately

FLUTE

YET NOT I BUT THROUGH CHRIST IN ME

FLUTE

© 2018 INTEGRITY'S ALLELUIA! MUSIC (SESAC), FARREN LOVE AND WAR PUBLISHING (SESAC)
and CITYALIGHT MUSIC (APRA) and Admin. at INTEGRATEDRIGHTS.COM
All Rights Reserved   Used by Permission

Words and Music by MICHAEL FARREN,
JONNY ROBINSON and RICH THOMPSON

Worship Ballad

YOU ARE MY KING

(Amazing Love)

FLUTE

© 1999 WORSHIPTOGETHER.COM SONGS (ASCAP)
Admin. at CAPITOLCMGPUBLISHING.COM
All Rights Reserved   Used by Permission

Words and Music by
BILLY JAMES FOOTE

YOUR GRACE IS ENOUGH

FLUTE

Words and Music by
MATT MAHER

© 2003, 2004 THANKYOU MUSIC (PRS) and SPIRITANDSONGCOM PUBLISHING (BMI)
THANKYOU MUSIC Admin. Worldwide at CAPITOLCMGPUBLISHING.COM excluding Europe which is Admin. by
 INTEGRITY MUSIC, part of the DAVID C COOK family. SONGS@INTEGRITYMUSIC.COM
SPIRITANDSONGCOM PUBLISHING Admin. by
 SONY MUSIC PUBLISHING (US) LLC, 424 Church Street, Suite 1200, Nashville, TN 37219
All Rights Reserved   Used by Permission

YOUR NAME

FLUTE

© 2006 INTEGRITY'S HOSANNA! MUSIC (ASCAP) and INTEGRITY WORSHIP MUSIC (ASCAP)
Admin. at INTEGRATEDRIGHTS.COM
All Rights Reserved   Used by Permission

Words and Music by PAUL BALOCHE
and GLENN PACKIAM

Moderately slow